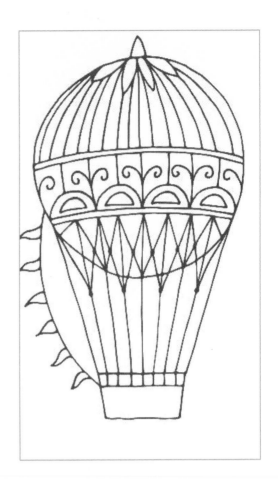

Professional Use Sketchbook

With heavy cream sketch paper, your designs, artwork and drawings will be created on heavy duty pages. This sketchbook may be used with pencil, sketch lead pencils, colored pencils, pen, gel pen, marker and paint. If paint is utilized, for best results remove page or lay open to dry overnight. Create with typography, doodle making, drawing, comic story layout, sketching or simply as a notebook.

Color Pallet

Choose your colors and mark a splotch of all colors on a single page. Place colors near and mix colors until desired result is achieved. Mixing colors and shading are an important part of the artistic creative process.

Doodle

Pen & Ink Drawings

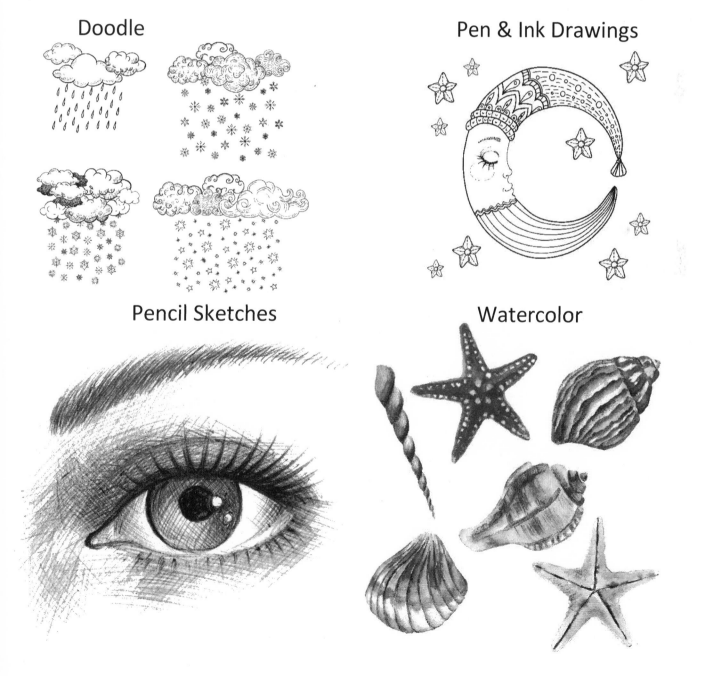

Pencil Sketches

Watercolor

Aa Bb Cc Dd Ee
Ff Gg Hh Ii Jj
Kk Ll Mm Nn Oo
Pp Qq Rr Ss Tt
Uu Vv Ww Xx
Yy Zz

Date: _____ Title: _____

Date: _____ Title: _____

Date: _____ Title: _____

Date: _____ Title: _____

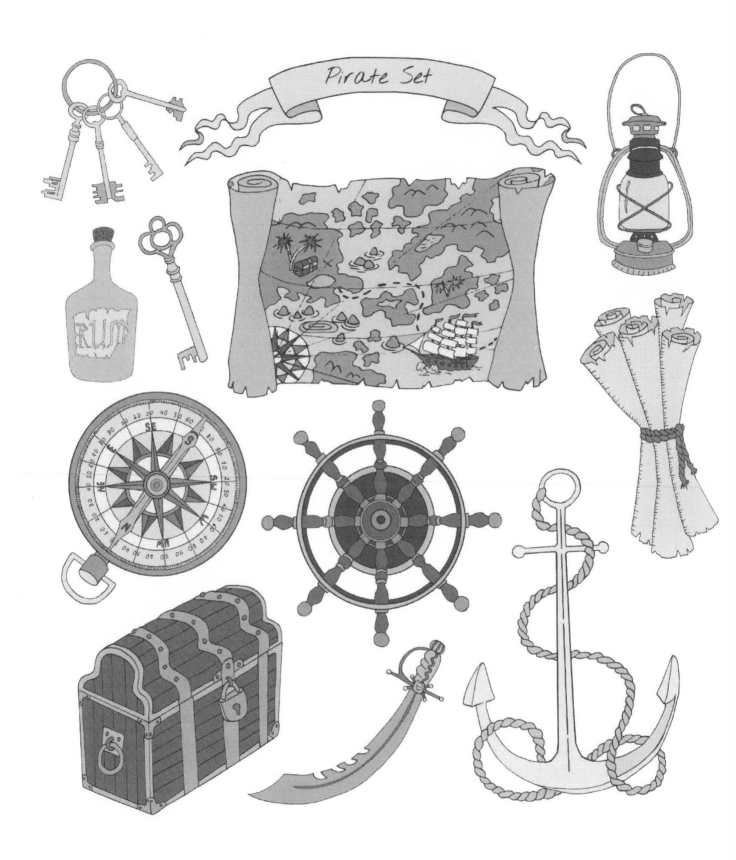

Pirate Set

Date: _____ Title: _____

Date: _____ Title: _____

Date: _____ Title: _____

Date: _____ Title: _____

Date: _____ Title: _____

Date: _____ Title: _____

Date: _____ Title: _____

Date: _____ Title: _____

Date: _____ Title: _____

Date: _____ Title: _____

Date: _____ Title: _____

Date: _____   Title: _____

Date: _____ Title: _____

Date: _____ Title: _____

Date: _____ Title: _____

Date: _____ Title: _____

Date: _____ Title: _____

Date: _____ Title: _____

Date: _____ Title: _____

Date: _____ Title: _____

Date: _____ Title: _____

Date: _____ Title: _____

Date: _____ Title: _____

Date: _____ Title: _____

Date: _____ Title: _____

Date: _____ Title: _____

Date: _____ Title: _____

Date: _____   Title: _____

Date: _____ Title: _____

Date: _____ Title: _____

Date: _____ Title: _____

Date: _____ Title: _____

Date: _____ Title: _____

Date: _____ Title: _____

Date: _____ Title: _____

Date: _____ Title: _____

Date: _____ Title: _____

To find more of our Sweet!ART instructional art classes, Sketchbooks, Notebooks and Journals simply search SWEET!ART Sketchbooks on AMAZON.com or Barnes & Noble.com. We thank you for your purchase.

Made in the USA
Columbia, SC
10 April 2019